GROUNDBREAKERS

Albert Einstein

Struan Reid

Heinemann
LIBRARY

www.heinemann.co.uk
Visit our website to find out more information about **Heinemann Library** books.

To order:
 Phone 44 (0) 1865 888066
 Send a fax to 44 (0) 1865 314091
Visit the Heinemann Bookshop at www.heinemann.co.uk to browse our catalogue and order online.

First published in Great Britain by Heinemann Library,
Halley Court, Jordan Hill, Oxford OX2 8EJ
a division of Reed Educational and Professional Publishing Ltd.
Heinemann is a registered trademark of Reed Educational & Professional Publishing Ltd.

OXFORD MELBOURNE AUCKLAND
JOHANNESBURG BLANTYRE GABORONE
IBADAN PORTSMOUTH (NH) USA CHICAGO

Designed by AMR
Illustrated by Art Construction
Originated by Ambassador Litho Ltd
Printed in Hong Kong/China

ISBN 0 431 10444 1
04 03 02 01 00
10 9 8 7 6 5 4 3 2 1

British Library Cataloguing in Publication Data
Reid, Struan
  Albert Einstein. – (Groundbreakers)
  1.Einstein, Albert, 1879–1955 – Juvenile literature
  2.Physicists – Germany – Biography – Juvenile literature
  I.Title
  530'.092

Acknowledgements
The publishers would like to thank the following for permission to reproduce photographs:
AKG Photo: pp. 6, 7, 8, 10/Erich Lessing, 11, 13, 15, 18/Erich Lessing, 20, 21, 22, 23, 24, 28, 29, 30, 40; Camera Press: pp. 4/Interfoto, 39/Alan Richards; Corbis: pp. 31/Bettmann, 33, 34; Hulton Getty: pp. 14, 32, 36; J. Allan Cash Ltd: pp. 9, 19; Mary Evans Picture Library: pp. 5, 35; Retrograph: p. 38; Science Photo Library: pp. 12/Sheila Terry, 25/John Sandford, 37, 41/Fermilab, 43/NASA

Our thanks to Patrick Fullick for his comments in the preparation of this book.

Every effort has been made to contact copyright holders of any material reproduced in this book. Any omissions will be rectified in subsequent printings if notice is given to the publishers.

Any words appearing in the text in bold, **like this**, are explained in the glossary.

Contents

The Universe explained

There are many stories about Albert Einstein the absent-minded professor, totally absorbed in his work and oblivious to every-day concerns. With his baggy trousers, shock of white, untidy hair and droopy moustache, he certainly looked the part. But he is also regarded as the greatest scientist of the 20th century, his face instantly recognizable throughout the world.

New questions and surprising answers

Einstein is famous for his theories of relativity, which turned upside down the beliefs about **gravity** and many other scientific laws that had been accepted for hundreds of years. His work changed for ever people's understanding of the Universe. His theories blew apart existing scientific beliefs and replaced them with answers to questions that had been puzzling scientists for centuries.

Einstein's first theory of relativity was published in 1905. The very next day, Einstein was being hailed as a genius and would remain famous for the rest of his life. He lived for another 50 years and wherever he went people flocked to see him, attracted by his fame.

> *'One of the greatest achievements in the history of human thought.'*
>
> (A scientist in 1905 describing Einstein's first theory of relativity)

Albert Einstein, whose theories answered questions that had been puzzling scientists for centuries.

Revolutionary

Einstein's theories were so revolutionary that not everyone accepted them immediately. Most people found them extremely difficult to understand, and many still do today. They were aware that his work had opened up completely new ways of explaining the Universe. However, while his discoveries gave many new answers, they also raised questions about long-held certainties such as time and space, which made people feel very unsure. They began to wonder whether the Universe has a beginning and what lies beyond. There had always been fixed answers to fixed questions but now everything seemed to be in doubt.

LA DOMENICA DEL CORRIERE

Supplemento settimanale illustrato del nuovo CORRIERE DELLA SERA - Abbonamenti: Italia, anno L. 1165, sem. L. 625 - Estero, anno L. 1765, sem. L. 925

Anno 52 — N. 3   15 Gennaio 1950   L. 25,—

Le formule misteriose del "mago": Alberto Einstein, creatore della teoria della relatività che ha aperto la via all'utilizzazione dell'energia atomica, ha enunciato nei giorni scorsi, in una lezione tenuta a Princeton, una nuova geniale teoria sulla concezione dell'universo (vedi altre notizie a pag. 4).

Einstein's face was recognized throughout the world. Here he appears on the cover of an Italian magazine of 1950.

Although Einstein's discoveries were beyond the understanding of many people, he had other strongly held beliefs that most people could understand – as a campaigner for world peace and a champion of truth and justice.

In Charlie Chaplin's words:

'The people are applauding you because none of them understands you, and applauding me because everybody understands me.'

(Reported to have been said by the comedian Charlie Chaplin to Einstein when driving in a car with him)

Early life

The town of Ulm in southern Germany today. Einstein's father was a businessman in the town and many of their relatives lived in the area.

Albert Einstein was born on 14 March 1879 in the southern German town of Ulm. He was the first child and only son of Hermann and Pauline Einstein. Their new baby boy had an unusual-shaped head and an overweight body, and when Pauline's mother Jette Koch saw her new grandson, she cried out: 'Much too fat! Much too fat!' A doctor reassured Albert's parents that their son would develop normally, and within a few months his body had grown to a proper size, but the back of his skull would always be an odd shape.

Hidden talents

Einstein's father, Hermann, was an electrical engineer with a small electrochemical factory in Ulm. But his business was not going well, and when his son was 1 year old, he moved with his family from Ulm to the nearby city of Munich. There, Hermann went into business with his brother Jacob making electrical instruments and equipment. The family shared a large, comfortable house with Jacob on the edge of the city. But Hermann was never a successful businessman.

Albert was taught at home until he was 7 years old and then he was sent to school. But he did not shine. He was quiet and shy and never enjoyed sports, preferring to sit alone and read.

Hermann and Pauline Einstein created a warm, friendly home for their children, Albert and his sister Maja, who was two and a half years younger. Pauline was a talented musician and she gave Albert violin lessons. These instilled a love of music in him that was to remain with him for the rest of his life, giving him peace and enjoyment. The Einsteins were Jewish, but they never followed the Jewish religious customs. However, Albert was always aware of the power and majesty of nature and the fact that there might be some 'other power' much greater than humans.

Albert's quiet, reserved exterior hid an inquisitive and determined mind. While he was growing up, many new scientific discoveries and mechanical inventions were being made. Albert was developing interests of his own, particularly in **algebra**. He was encouraged by his uncle Jacob and by a young student called Max Talmud, whom Albert's parents had befriended and who lent him books on science and philosophy.

Albert Einstein at the age of 5, with his sister Maja aged $2\frac{1}{2}$. This photograph was taken when the family was living in Munich.

Pauline Einstein

Pauline Einstein was the daughter of Julius Koch, a baker from Cannstatt in Germany who had made a fortune in the grain trade. She was intensely proud of her two children and encouraged them to work hard. She believed strongly in the education of women and was overjoyed when her daughter Maja later achieved a university degree in languages. At this time it was still unusual for women to continue their education beyond school.

A new nationality

In 1894, the Einstein family business collapsed and Albert's parents and sister moved to Milan in Italy, as business prospects looked more promising there. Albert was now 15 years old and was left behind to complete his school education in Munich. He hated being separated from his family and in the following year, 1895, left Munich and joined his family in Milan.

Disappointment into triumph

Hermann and Pauline were disappointed and angry that their son had dropped out of school before gaining proper qualifications. Hermann wanted his son to get a decent job, probably in electrical engineering. But Albert was determined to be a philosophy teacher, even though he had spoiled his chances of a place at university by leaving school early. His father finally persuaded him to study for something more practical. Albert applied for a course in electrical engineering at the Institute of Technology in Zurich, Switzerland, a college with an international reputation.

Albert studied hard for the entrance examination to the Zurich Institute. When he was not studying, he helped out in the new electrical business his family had started in Milan. But his parents were surprised and shocked when, in 1895, Albert failed the exam. He was awarded high marks for mathematics and physics, but failed dismally in subjects that did not interest him, such as French, chemistry and biology.

The Institute of Technology in Zurich, Switzerland, where Albert studied from 1896 until 1900.

Despite this failure, however, the staff at the Institute were so impressed by his mathematics and physics grades that they suggested he try the exam again and they would admit him. Albert therefore went to study for a year at a school in Aarau, a small town 40 kilometres (25 miles) west of Zurich. He was 16.

Albert gained dazzling marks and was awarded a diploma in 1896 that entitled him to enrol directly at the Zurich Institute without having to take the entrance examination again. The same year, he renounced his German citizenship as he felt more at home in Switzerland and was planning to apply for Swiss nationality.

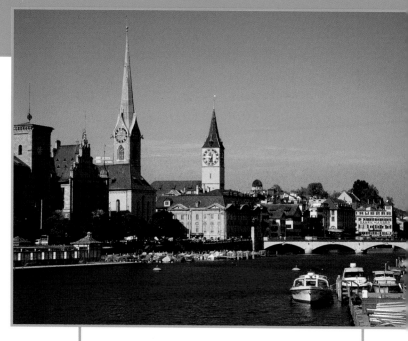

The city of Zurich today.

Fresh start

Albert now began a four-year course at the Zurich Institute, to qualify as a teacher in mathematics and physics. However, he found the course boring and did not always attend the lectures. He was disappointed that the lecturers seemed to ignore the latest scientific developments.

Albert made a number of close friends at the Institute. They discussed mathematics, attended concerts and enjoyed each other's company. Two of these friends in particular, Marcel Grossman and Angelo Besso, remained close to Albert for the rest of their lives. But he still took little interest in his work. However, Grossman lent him his own lecture notes and, with his help, Albert graduated in August 1900 with top grades. The following year, at the age of 22, he was finally granted Swiss citizenship.

Mileva Maric

Mileva Maric was also studying science and mathematics at the Institute while Albert was there and was the only woman in the classes. This was very unusual at that time, as very few women went on to study for further education. She came from Bacska in what is now Serbia. Einstein became very friendly with her and they were eventually to marry. But his friends and family were surprised at his interest in her – she was four years older than Einstein and seemed to have little sense of humour.

> *'You are a smart boy, Einstein, a very smart boy. But you have one great fault: you do not let yourself be told anything.'*
>
> (Heinrich Weber, Professor of Physics at the Zurich Institute)

9

Early career

Albert was now qualified as a mathematics and physics teacher. He was keen to start work as a lecturer but he found it very hard to find any work at all. His difficulties with his lecturers at the Institute meant that he could not apply for a job there.

Signs of promise

Albert eventually found some work as a temporary schoolteacher in Switzerland, first in a town called Winterthur and then in the capital city of Berne. He loved the work and derived great satisfaction from sharing his knowledge with his pupils. When he was not teaching, he continued with his own research in physics and also started writing articles for scientific journals. This enabled him to publish his ideas on some of the scientific mysteries of the day, ideas that would astound the world a few years later.

Increasingly frustrated and disappointed, Einstein felt that his career plans were being blocked wherever he looked. But once again his friend from his student days, Marcel Grossmann, came to his assistance. Marcel's father was very influential in Switzerland and recommended Albert for a job in the **Patent** Office in Berne. He was accepted.

Albert Einstein's desk at the Patent Office in Berne, where he worked on the theory of relativity.

On 23 June 1902, Albert began work as a Technical Expert (Third Class) in the Berne Patent Office. He was a low-grade clerk, part of a team of twelve, and his work involved inspecting and registering applications for patents from Swiss inventors. Many people would have found the work dull and repetitive, but Albert enjoyed it and his work hours also allowed him to continue with his own interests and researches. He was still writing and publishing scientific papers.

Marriage

With a secure job and a regular income, Albert was now in a position to get married. He and Mileva had been seeing a lot of each other and they shared many interests, particularly their love of mathematics. But Albert's parents, especially his mother, were against the relationship, as they had never liked Mileva. In fact, Pauline Einstein believed that Mileva must have cast a spell on her son! Despite this opposition from Albert's family, the couple were married on 6 January 1903. He was 23 years old and she was 27. They were to have three children – a girl, Lieserl, born in 1903 and later adopted by another family as she was born before they were married; Hans Albert, born in 1904; and Eduard, born in 1910. Eduard was to suffer from mental illness as an adult.

Einstein and Mileva with their baby son Hans Albert, photographed in 1904.

The Olympia Academy

At this time, Albert and some of his friends met regularly in each other's houses and went on walking holidays together. They called themselves 'The Olympia Academy'. They discussed the latest scientific research, philosophy and literature. 'Our means were frugal but our joy was boundless,' one of the group, Maurice Solovine, was to write later.

Motion, distance and time

Sir Isaac Newton. He was only 24 years old when he produced his theories that would dominate physics until 1905.

Until the end of the 19th century, most physicists based their work on the theories of the famous English scientist Isaac Newton (1642–1727). In 1687, Newton published a very influential book entitled *The Mathematical Principles of Natural Philosophy*, usually known by its shortened Latin name of the *Principia*. This work included his three Laws of Motion. These are rules that relate force and **gravity** and explain the principles that underlie the movement of all objects, on Earth and in space.

Questions …

Newton's Laws of Motion have had a major influence on scientific thinking up to the present day. But scientists began to ask new questions which these laws could not answer fully. For example, if everything is constantly moving, as Newton's laws claim, how is it possible to measure exact distances between objects and the exact time between events?

… and answers

The work of two American scientists, Edward Morley (1838–1923) and Albert Michelson (1852–1931), went some way towards answering this question. In 1887, they performed an experiment to measure the speed of light. They thought that if they were able to measure this, then they would have a fixed point against which other distances and events could be measured.

Morley and Michelson based their experiment on the work of a 19th-century Scottish scientist called James Clerk Maxwell. He believed that light was a form of **electromagnetic wave** that travelled through a mysterious light-carrying substance called the 'ether' that filled the whole of space. Morley and Michelson suggested that it should be possible to detect differences in the speed of light in different directions as the Earth was moving through the ether.

The American physicist Albert Michelson in old age. The experiment he did with Edward Morley raised questions that Einstein answered with the special theory of relativity.

They reflected beams of light from mirrors, so that some of the light travelled in the same direction as the Earth was moving in, and some travelled at right angles to this direction. They measured how long light took to travel in each direction, and checked their results by rotating the apparatus to change the direction in which each beam of light travelled.

Shock wave

However, Morley and Michelson could detect no differences in the speed of light. Instead, the speed of light appeared to be the same in whatever direction they measured it. This result shook the scientific world because it showed that while Newton's ideas explained movement on Earth, they could not be applied to the whole Universe. Eight years later, Einstein was able to explain exactly what was happening.

The miraculous year

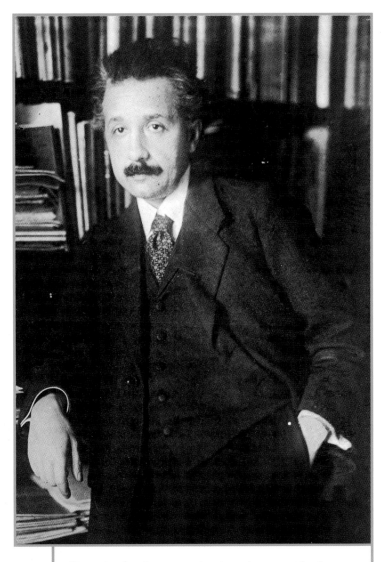

Einstein the famous scientist, photographed some years after the publication of his general theory of relativity.

The first few years of Albert's marriage were happy and contented. In 1905, a year that was to become known as his year of miracles, he published three new scientific papers, all of which were to prove extraordinary. 'Ideas come from God,' said Albert.

Atoms and photons

One of Albert's papers discussed the movement of tiny **particles** known as **atoms**. Until then, many scientists were uncertain whether atoms really existed. Nearly 80 years earlier, in 1827, the **botanist** Robert Brown noted that dust particles on the surface of water are always moving in all directions. This movement of particles came to be known as *Brownian motion*, even though Brown was unable to explain why it was happening.

ROBERT BROWN

Robert Brown (1773–1858) was a Scottish botanist who carried out many studies with a microscope. He collected 4000 plant **species** and spent five years classifying them. In 1827, the year that he discovered Brownian motion, he became keeper of the new botanical department at the British Museum.

Using mathematical equations, Albert showed that the **molecules** in a liquid bump into the dust particles on the surface, making the particles move quickly as if alive.

Three years later, in 1908, the French scientist Jean Perrin made detailed studies of Brownian motion. He studied the movement of particles in water and his results showed that Einstein's mathematical equations had been correct. Perrin's experiments provided the first evidence that atoms and molecules really do exist.

Albert's second paper of 1905 contained his ideas about the energy from light turning into electrical energy. He said that light consisted of tiny 'packets' of energy, which he called *photons*. Adapting an idea first developed in 1900 by a German scientist called Max Planck, he showed that when light shines on to a metal surface, **electrons** are knocked out of the metal atoms by the light photons, which produces an electric current. This is known as the *photoelectric effect*.

Max Planck, the German scientist who was to have a major influence on physics. He was Professor of Physics at various times at Kiel, Berlin and Munich universities.

MAX PLANCK

Max Planck (1858–1947) was born in Kiel, Germany. He studied physics at Munich University, where he later became a professor. In 1900, he published a scientific paper that introduced the idea of 'quantizing energy'. This stated that energy, such as light, was not continuous. Instead, energy existed in the form of tiny units that he called *quanta*. This idea led to the development of **quantum mechanics**, a new set of laws describing how atomic particles behave. In 1919, Planck was awarded the **Nobel Prize** for Physics for his discovery that energy is quantized.

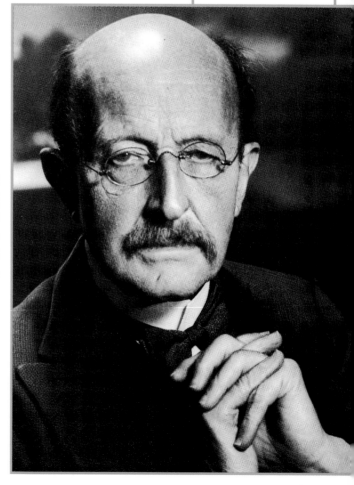

The special theory of relativity

Of the three scientific papers Albert published in 1905, the most astounding of all was the one on his special theory of relativity. It is known as 'special' because it applies to certain special conditions. It was published in June and contained Einstein's explanation for the baffling results from the 1887 light experiment by Morley and Michelson. It rocked the scientific world because it completely overturned Isaac Newton's view of fixed measurements of time and motion.

What is it?

In the special theory of relativity, Einstein showed that all movement is relative – all we can measure is how fast we are moving in relation to something else. Although the mathematical details of the special theory of relativity are extremely complicated, the main idea can be explained quite simply.

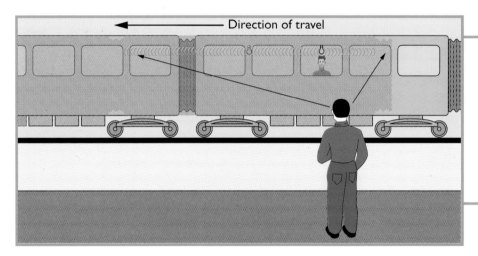

Diagram explaining Einstein's special theory of relativity, which showed there is no universal, absolute time.

Imagine that a train is moving out of a station. A flashing light bulb is suspended from the exact centre of the carriage ceiling. This sends out two flashes of light at exactly the same time but in opposite directions. If you were inside the carriage, you would see the light flashes reach the two ends of the carriage at exactly the same time. But if you were standing on the station platform, you would see something different as the train passes by. From the platform, the speed of both flashes of light is exactly the same as the light speed that you measure inside the train. However, as the light moves outwards from the bulb, the train is moving forwards.

From the platform, you would see the flash of light that is moving backwards hit the back wall of the carriage before seeing the forward-moving flash hit the front wall.

The speed of light is constant for all observers, whatever speed they are travelling at. But this example shows that an event – in this case the two light flashes hitting the end walls of the carriage – that one observer sees happen at exactly the same time, another observer (who is moving relative to the first observer) sees happen at different times.

With the special theory of relativity, Einstein showed that there is no universal, absolute time. Time, like motion, is relative to the observer. The only constant is the speed of light.

ONGOING IMPACT $E = mc^2$

Einstein's paper went on to say that there is a relation between the **mass** and energy of moving objects, which he expressed in what has become a famous equation, $E = mc^2$. This means that the energy (E) contained in any **particle** of **matter** is equal to its mass (m) multiplied by the square of the speed of light (c^2). In other words, tiny amounts of matter can be converted into enormous amounts of energy. This formula lies at the heart of all methods of obtaining **nuclear energy**.

TIME PASSES SLOWLY

As well as overturning Newton's idea of absolute time, the special theory of relativity predicted that the faster anything travels, the more slowly time will pass. For example, if an astronaut travels into space at nearly the speed of light, time will pass more slowly for the astronaut than for his or her twin back on Earth. When the astronaut returns to Earth, he or she will not be as old as the twin left behind on Earth.

The famous professor

The laboratory at Zurich University as it would have been at the time that Einstein taught there.

Following the publication of these amazing scientific papers, Einstein's name slowly became known to many scientists of the time. One of the first to show an interest in his work was Max Planck himself, who wrote asking for more information on the special theory of relativity. Einstein's old mathematics teacher from Zurich, Professor Hermann Minkowski, also took an interest in the theory. But while some scientists agreed with Einstein's work, many others dismissed it as nonsense.

Offers of work

In spite of growing interest in his scientific work, Einstein stayed in his job at the Berne **Patent** Office and was promoted to the position of Technical Expert (Second Class). He remained in this job for another five years. In 1908, he began teaching part-time at the University of Berne. Finally, in 1909 and aged 30, he resigned from the Patent Office.

HERMANN MINKOWSKI

The German mathematician Hermann Minkowski (1864–1909) had been Einstein's Professor of Mathematics at the Zurich Institute. Like many of Einstein's teachers there, he had clashed with the young student. However, it was he who developed Einstein's special theory of relativity. In 1908, he suggested that there are not three dimensions, but four – three dimensions in space and a fourth dimension in time. Einstein would later build upon this idea of space-time to develop his general theory of relativity in 1915.

The city of Prague in the Czech Republic. Einstein was appointed Professor of Physics at the university but stayed for less than a year.

He took up a permanent teaching position at the University of Zurich, but his lectures were never well attended because his teaching methods seemed very dull to the students. He found it difficult to convey complex ideas in an interesting way. However, the importance of his discoveries was now beginning to be recognized and offers of work from universities all over Europe came pouring in.

In 1911, Einstein was appointed Professor of Physics at the University of Prague (the capital of the present-day Czech Republic). With this new job came a good salary, and Einstein and his family moved into a comfortable new apartment in Prague. Einstein's new work enabled him to use the huge university libraries with their books and information on all the latest scientific discoveries. He was also in regular contact with many of the most important scientists of the day.

Hermann Minkowski was so impressed by Einstein's work that in 1907 he wrote:

'From now on space and time separately have vanished into the merest shadows, and only a sort of combination of the two preserves any reality.'

By this, Minkowski meant that the measurements of space and time could never be the same again.

Back to Germany

Einstein (far left) and fellow scientists. Einstein felt that he did his best work when his relationships with other people were going well.

The Einsteins were never very happy in Prague. They were there little more than a year before they moved back to Zurich, where Einstein was appointed Professor of Physics at his old college, the Zurich Institute. He was 33 years old and seventeen years had passed since, as a boy of 16, he had first failed the entrance examination to the college. Mileva was happier to be back in Zurich as they were among their old friends once more. One of these was Marcel Grossmann, who began helping Einstein to develop his work on the relativity theory. Einstein wrote at the time about this work: 'I occupy myself exclusively with the problem.'

Losing his family

Einstein stayed in Zurich for two years. In December 1913, he was offered a prize job at the University of Berlin in Germany, as the Research Director at the new Institute of Physics. This was a very exciting offer as it was an extremely important post and would provide Einstein with the ideal conditions for completing his work on relativity.

The city of Berlin in 1913, the year before Einstein started his job there as director of the newly created Kaiser Wilhelm Institute for Physics.

Einstein started working in Berlin in the spring of 1914, and in April Mileva and their two sons Hans Albert and Eduard joined him. But no sooner had they arrived than Mileva took them back to Zurich. She disliked living in Germany, and being in Berlin would mean that they were closer to her mother-in-law, Pauline Einstein, who had never accepted her. Einstein was very upset by their departure. However, for some time he and Mileva had been very unhappy together, and it was now obvious that their marriage was coming to an end.

Mileva and the two boys moved into a rented apartment in Zurich, and Mileva had to give piano and mathematics lessons to help pay the rent. Although he was separated from his sons, Einstein was happy in Berlin and could now concentrate on his work. He later described Berlin as the place he 'felt closely connected to by human and scientific relations'.

Mileva's contribution

Since first meeting as students in Zurich, Mileva had been a valuable source of support and information for her husband's work. They spent many hours together discussing their ideas. When Einstein won the 1921 **Nobel Prize** for Physics, he gave the prize money ($35,000) to Mileva to support herself and their sons. But Mileva became very bitter and claimed much of the credit for Einstein's success. She was without doubt a great help to Einstein in the early years of their marriage, but whether she contributed directly to his work is debatable.

The First World War

When Einstein moved back to Germany – the country of his birth – at the beginning of 1914, his prospects looked promising. But the storm clouds were already gathering as one of the most destructive wars ever to be fought was soon to explode across the face of Europe.

A German First World War poster. The government appeals to the German people's national pride and family values to fight the war.

A world gone mad

On 1 August 1914, the First World War broke out between Germany, Austria and their allies on one side, and Britain, France and Russia and their allies on the other. Many people on both sides greeted the outbreak of war with enthusiasm, as they believed that they would be fighting for freedom and justice. But Einstein believed that the war was unnecessary and, indeed, was sheer destructive madness. He was especially angered by the work of the scientists who invented terrible new weapons, such as poisonous gas. He believed this was an abuse of science.

A year after the outbreak of war, Einstein signed a document called the Manifesto to Europeans, along with many other famous people in Germany and elsewhere. This was an appeal to everyone who valued 'the culture of Europe' to come to their senses and form an association of countries.

This 'league of nations' would be dedicated to the promotion of peace between nations. By signing this manifesto, Einstein publicly declared himself a **pacifist** against war. From now on until his death, he would actively support peaceful actions to settle disputes, and campaign for justice and tolerance. At the same time, Einstein joined a political party that tried to end the war. This was banned by the German government in 1916.

Some time away

In the summer of 1915, Einstein went on holiday to a remote island in the Baltic Sea. He followed this trip with a visit to his sons in Zurich and he took Hans Albert walking and boating in southern Germany.

Before returning to Berlin, Einstein visited a French writer and fellow pacifist, Romain Rolland, who lived near Lake Geneva in Switzerland.

In a fellow pacifist's words:

'He [Einstein] is very much alive and fond of laughter. He cannot help giving an amusing twist to the most serious thoughts … He is one of the very few men whose spirit had remained free among the general servility.'

(The pacifist Romain Rolland on meeting Einstein on 6 September 1915)

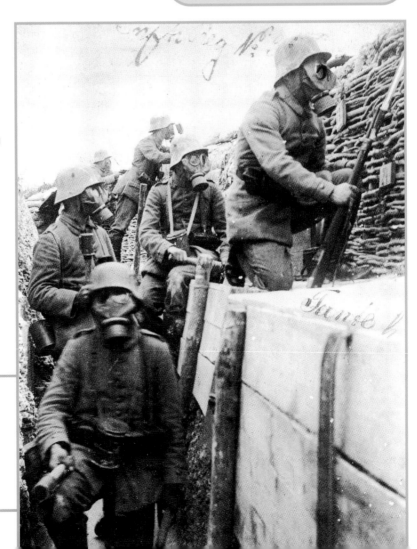

Trench warfare during the First World War. The use of poisonous gases by the Germans outraged Einstein.

Reaching the goal

While he was campaigning for peace and becoming involved in political issues, Einstein continued with his scientific research. During the war years, from 1914 until 1918, he wrote over 50 scientific papers and published a book. He was also becoming increasingly famous and, wherever he went, crowds turned out to greet him. Switzerland remained neutral throughout the war, and Einstein's Swiss passport meant that he could travel, despite the war. He visited other scientists and **pacifists** in Switzerland and Holland. He was invited to address scientific meetings and, at last, more scientists were beginning to take his ideas more seriously.

Too little time

During the autumn of 1915, Einstein missed meals and worked late into the night. When he did eat, he cooked everything together in the same pot to save time and trouble. One day, his future stepdaughter Margot found him boiling an egg in some soup, planning to eat both. His health suffered as a result of these bad eating habits, but as always his work came first and he continued with his research.

Einstein and his stepdaughter Margot.

Gradually, Einstein came closer and closer to his goal. At the end of November 1915, he finally worked out the answer he had been searching for since ten years earlier. At last, he had discovered how to include the effects of **gravity** in the relativity theory. It was as if he had been feeling his way through darkness and had suddenly come out into brilliant sunshine.

A new beginning

The general theory of relativity completely changed the way in which we understand the world. For 200 years, many of the most important problems in physics had been explained using Newton's laws. The general theory now replaced Newton's work. It provided a revolutionary new means to explore and understand our Universe, explaining its origin and destiny.

Some people were alarmed by these discoveries as they felt that they could not even rely on the evidence of their own eyes any more. But others were excited and felt inspired by feelings of awe and wonder at the fantastic laws of nature that Einstein had revealed. His discoveries also had a great effect on the work of writers, artists and philosophers.

Night sky with stars and planets. Einstein's general theory of relativity explained many of the mysteries of the Universe.

In March 1916, Einstein published his general theory of relativity. His friend, the physicist Max Born, described this as

'a great work of art … the greatest feat of human thinking about nature'.

The general theory of relativity

Like the special theory of relativity, Einstein's general theory of relativity is extremely complicated. But we can explain the main ideas contained in this theory quite simply.

In the general theory of relativity, Einstein writes that space is warped or 'curved' by objects and that the more massive the object, the greater this effect is. The extent of this warping or curvature of space is greatest near the object, and becomes progressively less as the distance from the object increases.

Imagine space as a flat rubber sheet. If a heavy rock is placed in the centre of the sheet, the rubber will warp or sag in the middle. The heavier the rock, the greater the sag. If a ball is rolled across the rubber sheet, it will go down the slope towards the rock. The closer it gets to the rock, the more the ball will be pulled down towards it. If it passes very close to the rock, the ball will circle, or orbit, the rock repeatedly. In the same way, our Universe, **radiation** and material objects are pulled in by the curvature of space near massive objects. That is why the Earth orbits the Sun, and the Moon orbits the Earth.

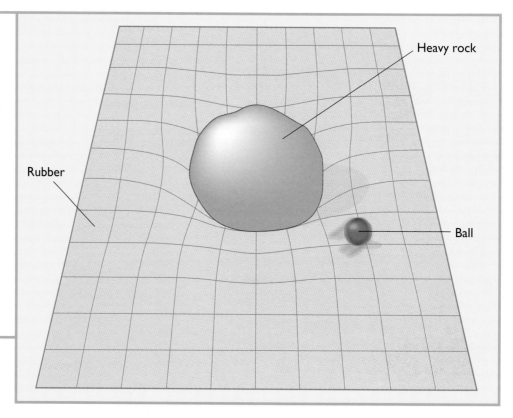

Diagram explaining the general theory of relativity. Space is warped closest to the massive object, where there is the greatest gravitational pull.

Heavy rock

Rubber

Ball

The general theory of relativity also states that light has **mass** and would therefore be affected by **gravity**. For example, starlight passing close to the Sun should be pulled towards the Sun, following the curvature in space caused by the Sun's mass. Einstein hoped that astronomers would be able to test this theory.

Proving the theory

Following the publication in 1916 of Einstein's general theory, the opportunity to test it arose three years later, in 1919, when there was an eclipse of the Sun. The bending of light by gravity that Einstein predicted was detected by photographing two stars during the eclipse. A team of astronomers led by an English physicist called Arthur Eddington measured the position of the stars. As the light rays from the stars passed the Sun, they were 'bent' by its field of gravity. As a result, to the astronomers the two stars appeared to be further apart than usual.

Diagram that shows how gravity bends light. The path of the starlight is bent by the Sun's gravity.

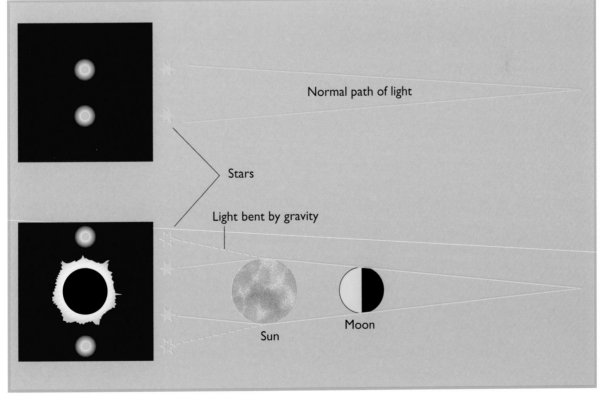

Normal path of light

Stars

Light bent by gravity

Sun

Moon

International acclaim

Einstein and his cousin Elsa Lowenthal shortly after their marriage in 1919. They were to remain together until Elsa's death in 1936.

The year 1916, in which Einstein published his general theory of relativity, also marked the end of the period of his greatest work. He had been working extremely hard – in just one year he had produced ten scientific papers and a book that explained relativity – and he was exhausted. His marriage had broken down completely and the separation from his sons upset him. In 1917, Einstein fell seriously ill with a stomach ulcer. Weak and in great pain, he spent much of his time in bed. But even then he would work non-stop for long stretches.

New battles

Since moving to Berlin in 1914, Einstein had developed a close relationship with his cousin, Elsa Lowenthal. She persuaded him to move to an apartment near hers. Visiting him every day, she helped him back to health, cooking his meals and making sure that he kept to a strict diet. Elsa was divorced from her first husband and had two daughters. In February 1919, Einstein and Mileva were finally divorced and in the following June he married Elsa. They were together for seventeen years, until Elsa's death in 1936.

Einstein may have been more settled now in his home life, but this was a time of great unrest in Europe, especially in Germany. The First World War ended on 11 November 1918 with the surrender of Germany. But the fighting continued on the streets in Germany as the people battled among themselves for control of the country.

Enemies of the state

Following Germany's defeat in the First World War, many Germans looked around for people to blame. They blamed the newly formed and more free-thinking **Weimar Republic**, which they referred to as 'the Traitor Republic'. They also blamed the **pacifists** and Jews. People were denounced as 'traitors' if they had been pacifists during the war. As a Jew, Einstein also became the target of **anti-Semitic** Germans, who were angered by his campaign for peace and irritated by his growing fame throughout the world. He was also attacked by some of his German scientist colleagues. They were led by a physicist called Philipp Lenard, who talked about 'German physics' and criticized 'Jewish science'. He denounced Einstein as a supporter of peace, a socialist and a Jew.

Einstein out boating. Some of his happiest and most relaxing moments were when he was able to get away from his work and sail on lakes.

German scientists were generally unwelcome at scientific meetings after the end of the First World War. However, as a well-known supporter of peace, Einstein was welcomed wherever he went and he was invited to give lectures throughout Europe. Finally, in 1922, Einstein was awarded the 1921 **Nobel Prize** for Physics. However, this was not for his work on relativity. It was for his less important work on the photoelectric effect, which he had published in 1905.

A growing public role

During the 1920s, Einstein continued to give lectures around the world. As hostility towards him increased in Germany, he welcomed these trips abroad, and wherever he and Elsa went, the lecture halls were crowded with people. He received enthusiastic reports in newspapers and he was appointed guest lecturer at universities throughout the world.

The French newspaper *L'Humanité*, reporting on Einstein's visit to France, said:

'Everyone had the impression of being in the presence of a sublime genius.'

Science moves on

Einstein's views on politics and peace also made him a world-famous figure. The League of Nations had been founded in 1920 to try and maintain peace between nations and in 1922, Einstein became a member of the League's Committee on Intellectual Co-operation. In 1925, he campaigned for the abolition of compulsory military service.

*Einstein and fellow **pacifists** in Berlin in 1923. He was becoming more and more involved in the campaign of world disarmament.*

Niels Bohr. His work on quantum mechanics was to lead to many disagreements with Einstein, but they always remained close friends.

NIELS BOHR

Einstein also supported the Women's International League for Peace and Freedom, which called for international **disarmament**.

With his own, most important work behind him, Einstein now became involved in two other areas of physics – the unified field theory and **quantum mechanics**. But towards the end of the 1920s, his ideas were being overtaken by new research. Quantum mechanics describes the behaviour of the **particles** of **matter** that make up atoms – protons, neutrons and **electrons**. A number of new discoveries, notably by the New Zealand physicist Ernest Rutherford and the Danish physicist Niels Bohr, suggested that these particles behave randomly, by chance. This uncertainty contradicted everything that had been believed so far and Einstein could not accept it. 'God does not play dice,' he said. However, other leading physicists were beginning to accept the idea of chance, and even though his scientific reputation was untouchable, Einstein became increasingly isolated from new developments.

Niels Bohr (1885–1962) was born in Denmark, the son of a professor of **physiology**. By 1913, he had devised a new model of the structure of the atom using the ideas of quantum mechanics. He showed that electrons move around the **nucleus** of the atom in different levels of set amounts of energy, sometimes called 'shells'. He won the 1922 **Nobel Prize** for Physics, the year after Einstein. He was against **Fascism** and when the Germans invaded Denmark in 1940, he escaped by boat to Sweden and then to the USA.

A change of life

Throughout the 1920s and into the early '30s, Einstein continued his campaign for world peace. In written articles and public lectures, he called on people to refuse to serve in their country's army, to stop producing weapons and to work for peace instead.

A Nazi rally marching through the streets of Berlin during the 1930s. The Nazi Party encouraged hatred towards anyone they regarded as enemies of Germany. The figure standing in the car is Adolf Hitler.

The politics of hate

At the same time as Einstein was calling for peace, a terrifying new character was emerging on the world stage – Adolf Hitler. He was supported by various groups of people in Germany who attacked anyone they regarded as enemies of their own distorted views of German patriotism.

These included religious leaders, scientists, artists and philosophers. They also whipped up anti-Jewish hysteria.

In 1933, Adolf Hitler and his **Nazi** Party came to power in Germany. Einstein and Elsa were visiting the USA at the time. In Einstein's absence, his scientific writings were attacked for being 'Jewish' and therefore un-German. His books were publicly burned, along with the works of other Jews, **pacifists** and anti-Nazis. Several peace campaigners were arrested and even imprisoned. Einstein's name was published on the first page of a list of 'enemies' of Germany.

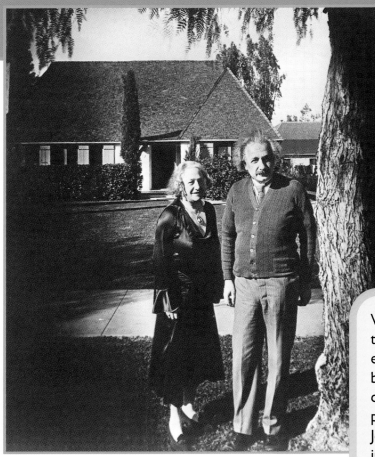

Elsa and Albert Einstein in front of their house in Pasadena, California. In 1931, two years before they left Germany for good, he was working at the California Institute of Technology.

Einstein emigrates

Realizing that his life was in danger, Einstein decided not to return to Germany. He stayed for a few months in Belgium and then England. On 17 October 1933, he and Elsa left Europe for a new life in the USA. Like many other Jews, he was never to return to Germany. The previous year, in 1932, the University of Princeton in the USA had offered Einstein the position of Professor of Physics at the **Institute for Advanced Study**. By the end of that year, he had made up his mind to accept, and from 1933 until his death 22 years later, Princeton was to be his home.

ZIONISM

With the increasing hostility shown to Jews in 1930s Germany and elsewhere in Europe, Einstein became involved in a movement called **Zionism**. Zionists were people who supported the claims of Jews to establish a Jewish homeland in the Middle East. This eventually happened in 1948 with the foundation of the state of Israel, which in turn displaced many thousands of native Palestinian people from their homeland. For the rest of his life, Einstein helped Jewish people in need and encouraged the teaching of science in the new state of Israel.

In Einstein's words:

'In the last analysis, everyone is a human being, irrespective of whether he is an American or a German, a Jew or a Gentile [non-Jew]. If it were possible to manage with this point of view, which is the only dignified one, I would be a happy man.'

(In a letter to the *New York Herald Tribune* newspaper in 1935)

The heart of the atom

*Robert Oppenheimer (1904–67),
nuclear physicist. From 1943 until
1945, he was director of the Los
Alamos laboratory, which produced
the first atomic bomb. He later
opposed the development of the
hydrogen ('H') bomb.*

In Einstein's words

Einstein believed that the
Nazis had to be stopped and
if this meant war, then it was
unavoidable. He wrote:

*'Organized power can be
opposed only by organized
power. Much as I regret this,
there is no other way.'*

The growing menace from **Nazi**
Germany and the attacks on
German Jews and anyone else
opposed to Nazi beliefs eventually
convinced Einstein that at certain
times war is necessary to stop
aggression. He still clung to his
ideals of world peace but saw that
for now this was not possible.
However, he was soon to be
involved with the most destructive
weapon in history.

A world dilemma

When the Second World War
broke out in 1939, Einstein and
other scientists wrote to Franklin D.
Roosevelt, president of the USA,
urging him to begin development of
an atomic bomb. Einstein knew that
German scientists had discovered
that huge amounts of energy were
released by splitting **atoms** and he
was afraid that they would draw
upon this knowledge and build an
atomic bomb first.

The atomic bomb was not invented
by Einstein, but it was his
$E = mc^2$ equation of 1905 that
stated the basic principle of the
bomb. When the USA entered the
war in 1942, President Roosevelt
set up what was called the
Manhattan Project to develop an
atomic bomb, following the advice
of Einstein and other scientists.

ENRICO FERMI

Enrico Fermi (1901–54) was the greatest Italian scientist of the 20th century. He studied at the University of Pisa and in 1938, as an opponent of **Fascism**, he left for the USA where he worked at Columbia University in New York. In 1942, he produced the first controlled nuclear reaction. Although he was involved in the development of the first atomic bombs, he opposed American plans to build another, more powerful bomb known as the hydrogen or 'H' bomb.

By the outbreak of the war, German scientists had discovered that if the **nucleus** of an atom was split in two, in a process called *nuclear fission*, an enormous amount of energy was released. If this energy were uncontrolled, there would be a massive explosion. In 1942, the Italian scientist Enrico Fermi built a device called a nuclear reactor in which he produced controlled **nuclear energy**.

*Enrico Fermi, who left Italy for the USA in protest against the policies of the Fascist government of Benito Mussolini. He was awarded the **Nobel Prize** for Physics in 1938.*

Japan

The first atomic bombs were developed under the supervision of US physicist Robert Oppenheimer, who was in charge of the Manhattan Project. Einstein knew when the first bombs were nearly ready for use in 1945. By then, the war with Germany was coming to an end and he wrote another letter to President Roosevelt urging him not to use the bombs. But the war with the Japanese still continued and in August 1945, believing that little else could persuade them to surrender, the USA dropped two bombs, on the Japanese cities of Hiroshima and Nagasaki. Many thousands of people were killed instantly, while many thousands more died slowly and painfully later from the effects of the bombs.

After the war

Once the war was over, Einstein returned to his campaign for peace and called even more vigorously for nuclear **disarmament**. 'The war is won,' he said, 'but the peace is not.' He realized the dangers that this new nuclear power posed. He had lived through two terrible world wars and was sickened by the mindless destruction they had caused.

New dangers

Einstein stepped up his campaign for peace, in letters, interviews, radio broadcasts and public speeches. He believed that a new world government should be created that would finally put an end to the rivalry between nations. He believed that this was the only answer for a world that was now on the brink of destruction by nuclear warfare. He wrote: 'Science has brought forth this danger but the real problem is in the hearts and minds of men.'

Einstein believed that while the huge amount of energy created by nuclear power should not be used for destructive purposes, it could be used to help the world. But even here, Einstein saw the dangers and warned that new science-based technology should be kept under very strict control in order to avoid the destruction of the world.

> **In Einstein's words:**
>
> *'all our … technological progress – our very civilization – is like an axe in the hand of a pathological criminal.'*
>
> (In a letter to a friend in 1917)

Einstein swears the oath of allegiance when he becomes a US citizen in 1940.

Physicists Otto Hahn and Lise Meitner. They worked together in Berlin during the 1930s until Meitner left Germany for Sweden.

These years after the war also brought family concerns to Einstein. For many years his youngest son Eduard had been mentally ill. Mileva was now also very ill and Einstein was receiving upsetting news about her and their son. He had always kept the promise he had made 25 years earlier to care for them financially and he sent her regular payments. These helped to pay for Eduard's expensive medical bills. Einstein had last seen his son in May 1933 and they were never to meet again. Eduard died in a psychiatric hospital in Switzerland in 1962, where he had been for 22 years.

Later life

In his later life, Einstein continued with his political work and the peace movement. He had become a US citizen in 1940, while still keeping his Swiss nationality. He was always grateful to the USA for the warm welcome he had received when he fled **Nazi** Germany in 1933. But his peace and justice campaign after the war made him unpopular with the US authorities. He championed the public's right to know about the important issues of the day, such as whether nuclear weapons were being made. He also believed that teachers should be allowed to discuss these matters with their students without fear of censorship.

Investigations

During the 1950s, Einstein was suspected of having **communist** sympathies and was investigated by the **FBI**. He now campaigned against the persecution of people suspected of having links with communists and of being involved in 'un-American activities'. Many of his friends and scientific colleagues were among those being investigated, including Robert Oppenheimer, who had been in charge of the Manhattan Project and was now Director of the **Institute for Advanced Study** at Princeton.

Einstein at a press conference in Pittsburgh, Pennsylvania, USA. He is being questioned about his scientific theories.

Einstein in reflective mood in 1944, when he was 66 years old.

EINSTEIN FOR PRESIDENT

Einstein's support for **Zionism** from the 1920s made him an extremely popular figure in the new state of Israel. He had been one of the founders of the Hebrew University in Jerusalem, which he had inaugurated in 1922. He was so famous and popular that, in 1952, he was invited to become President of Israel as a mark of gratitude for all he had done for the Jewish people. But Einstein wished to avoid the world of politics as much as possible. Einstein declined the invitation with the words: 'I am deeply moved by the offer … and at once saddened … because I cannot accept it. All my life I have dealt with objective matters. Hence, I lack both the natural aptitude and the experience to deal properly with people and to exercise official functions.'

Einstein continued with his scientific research and his fight for truth and justice until the very end. One day in April 1955, Einstein collapsed at home and was rushed to the Princeton hospital. His doctors believed he could be saved if he agreed to have an operation, but he replied, 'I do not believe in artificially prolonging life.' In the morning of 18 April, he died. He was 76. Beside his bed was a paper covered with his latest scientific calculations. His friend Alice Kahler, writing to a relative, said: 'The world has lost its best man, and we have lost our best friend. And it came so suddenly.'

Einstein's legacy

Images of Einstein such as this often occur in magazines, newspapers and other media, representing the 'face of science'.

In Einstein's words

This is part of Einstein's acceptance speech to the British Royal Astronomical Society when he was awarded its Gold Medal in 1925:

'He who finds a thought that lets us penetrate even a little deeper into the eternal mystery of nature has been granted great grace. He who, in addition, experiences the recognition, sympathy, and help of the best minds of his time, has been given almost more happiness than a man can bear.'

In 1949, he wrote: *'My scientific work is motivated by an irresistible longing to understand the secrets of nature and by no other feelings. My love for justice and striving to contribute towards the improvement of human conditions are quite independent of my scientific interests.'*

For much of his life, Einstein's fame was legendary. His achievements made him one of the greatest scientists ever. But as well as for his scientific genius, Einstein is also remembered today for his modesty, and his courage in his fight for world peace. He believed passionately that scientists should be fully responsible for their work and play their part in the world around them.

The face of science

Einstein was one of the founders of modern physics. He was the first scientist since Isaac Newton 200 years earlier to come up with new explanations of how the Universe works. Newton believed in 'absolute' space and time. Einstein showed that space and time are 'relative' measurements, which can be different when different people do the measuring, and that there is no such thing as a 'correct' measurement.

Today, Einstein's theories of relativity form the basis of modern science. The special theory was accepted after a few years, as it answered many of the questions that scientists were asking at that time. But the general theory took longer to be accepted because people then could not see its practical use. It was not until much later, in the 1960s, that new devices such as **particle accelerators** were able to test parts of the theory. In 1976, **laser** experiments between the Earth and the Moon supported the general theory.

The enormous impact that Einstein's discoveries have had on the world can be shown by the fact that his name and face alone have come to symbolize science throughout the world. In his later years, he was nearly as famous for his political campaigns as he was for his scientific research. But he himself regarded his scientific work as the most important, as it opened up some of the greatest secrets of our world and Universe.

In Robert Oppenheimer's words:

'There was always with him a wonderful purity at once childlike and profoundly stubborn'.

Inside a modern particle accelerator, which is used for research in nuclear physics.

Discoveries since Einstein

In his later years, Einstein searched for a theory that in one mathematical equation would bring together **gravity**, **electromagnetism** and many other kinds of forces. In this way, he hoped to open up the innermost secrets of the Universe to understand how it and everything in it works. Scientists today continue with his quest for one theory that connects, or unifies, everything. This is known as the 'grand unification theory'.

The origin of the Universe

In 1927, Belgian astronomer Georges Lemaître used Einstein's general theory of relativity to propose that the Universe was still expanding. He claimed that the Universe must have grown out of a tiny point of energy which exploded, and out of which came space, time and **matter**. This has become known as the 'Big Bang' theory and is now seen as the best explanation for the origin of the Universe. In 1964, two US astronomers called Robert Wilson and Arno Penzias picked up faint radio noise from space. This is now thought to be the echo of the Big Bang. As new discoveries have been made in space, the Big Bang theory has been refined and modified.

Diagram illustrating the Big Bang theory. After its creation approximately 10,000 million years ago, the Universe is still expanding.

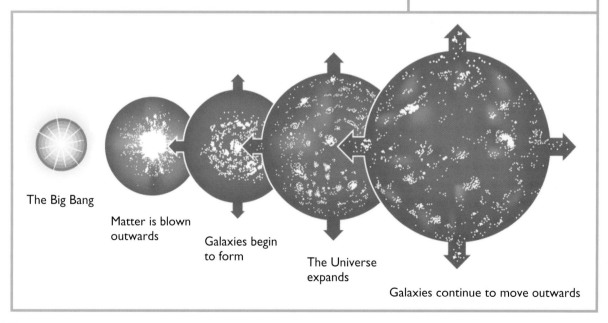

The Big Bang

Matter is blown outwards

Galaxies begin to form

The Universe expands

Galaxies continue to move outwards

The Hubble Telescope was launched in 1993 to investigate our galaxy.

In 1970, British scientists Roger Penrose and Stephen Hawking proved that if Einstein's general theory of relativity is correct, then it is possible that there was a definite beginning to the Universe. At this point, called a *singularity*, space and time as we know them would not have existed.

The future of the Universe

In 1983, physicists used the general theory to work out the history of the Universe back to a fraction of a second before the Big Bang. In 1993, the NASA satellite Cosmic Background Explorer (COBE) recorded the temperature of the afterglow of the Big Bang. Some scientists believe that in the far distant future, billions of years away, the Universe could collapse in on itself and then be reborn in another Big Bang. Others believe that it will continue to expand so that it fades away into a sea of **radiation**. But they are still inspired by Einstein in their search for a greater understanding of the Universe.

BLACK HOLES

Using Einstein's general theory of relativity, astronomers have found extraordinary objects far away in space, such as **pulsars**, **quasars** and black holes. In these situations, the force of gravity is extremely curved. A black hole occurs when matter becomes extremely dense, as in an exploded star. Around a black hole the fabric of space-time is very curved. Its gravity becomes so strong that both matter and radiation, including light, are trapped inside.

Astronomers today are also looking for galaxies that might be acting as '**gravitational lenses**'. Galaxies are much more massive than our Sun and they should bend light rays even more than was predicted by Einstein and proved in 1919.

Timeline

1879	Birth of Albert Einstein in Ulm, Germany.
1896	Albert begins a course at the Zurich Institute of Technology.
1900	Max Planck introduces the idea of 'quantizing energy'.
1901	Einstein is granted Swiss citizenship.
1902	Begins work at the Berne Patent Office.
1903	Marries Mileva Maric. Birth of daughter Lieserl.
1904	Birth of son Hans Albert.
1905	Einstein publishes three scientific papers, including one on his special theory of relativity.
1906	Writes his first paper on quantum mechanics.
1909	Resigns from the Patent Office and appointed an assistant professor at Zurich University, Switzerland.
1910	Birth of second son, Eduard.
1911	Marie Curie receives the Nobel Prize for Physics for her work on radioactivity, becoming the first person to win the prize twice. Ernest Rutherford shows that atoms have a central nucleus.
1913	Niels Bohr proposes a new model of the hydrogen atom.
1914	Einstein takes up the post of Research Director at the Institute of Physics, Berlin, Germany.
1915	Signs the Manifesto to Europeans, which calls for a league of nations to bring about peace.
1916	Publishes his general theory of relativity.
1919	Einstein and Mileva divorce. He marries Elsa Lowenthal.
1922	Einstein awarded the Nobel Prize for Physics for 1921.
1923	Edwin Hubble proves the existence of galaxies besides our own.
1927	Georges Lemaître proposes that the Universe is continually expanding.
1929	Hubble shows that galaxies are moving away from each other.
1933	The Einsteins leave Europe and settle in the USA.
1936	Death of Elsa Einstein.
1937	Otto Hahn announces discovery, with Lise Meitner, of nuclear fission.
1940	Einstein becomes an American citizen, but keeps his Swiss nationality.
1945	First nuclear bombs dropped, on Hiroshima and Nagasaki in Japan.
1948	Hermann Bondi and Thomas Gold propose the steady state theory of the Universe.

| 1949 | Francis Crick and James Watson discover the structure of DNA, the 'molecule of life'. |
| 1955 | Death of Albert Einstein. |

Places to visit and further reading

Places to visit

Science Museum, London
The Planetarium, London
Royal Observatory, Greenwich, London
Jodrell Bank Science Centre, Macclesfield
Woolsthorpe Manor, Lincolnshire (Isaac Newton's house)
Musée de l'Observatoire, Paris
Sammlung Warburg im Planetarium, Hamburg
Deutsches Museum, Munich
Space Center, Alamogordo, New Mexico
Science and Technology Museum of Atlanta, Georgia
National Air and Space Museum, Washington, DC

Websites

Science Museum Homepage:
   www.nmsi.ac.uk
European Laboratory for Particle Physics:
   www.cern.ch

Further reading

Angliss, Sarah: *Cosmic Journeys* – Future Files series (Franklin Watts, London, 1997)
Dolan, Graham: *The Greenwich Guide to Time and the Millenium* (Heinemann Library, Oxford, 1999)
Donkin, Andrew: *The Cosmic Professor: The Story of Albert Einstein* (Hodder Wayland, London, 1997)
Macdonald, Fiona: *Albert Einstein* – The World in the Time of ... series (Belitha, London, 1998)
Oxlade, Chris: *Earth and Beyond* – Science Topics series (Heinemann Library, Oxford, 1998)

Glossary

algebra branch of mathematics in which letters or other symbols are used to represent numbers

anti-Semitism persecution of or discrimination against people of Semitic (usually thought to be Jewish) origin

atom the smallest particle of an element. The atoms of many elements are bound together in groups to form particles called molecules.

botanist someone who studies plants

communist supporter of communism, the idea that there should be no classes in society and that no one should own anything privately, that workers help create wealth and therefore should own the means of producing that wealth

disarmament the reduction by a country or a state of its weapons and armed forces

electromagnetic wave a form of energy. Gamma rays, X-rays, ultraviolet, visible light, infra-red, microwaves and radio waves are all types of electromagnetic waves.

electromagnetism magnetism produced by electric current

electron a particle that orbits the nucleus in an atom. It has a negative electric charge.

Fascism political movement started by Benito Mussolini in Italy. It put nation and race before individuals and democracy.

FBI abbreviation for the Federal Bureau of Investigation. This is an agency of the US Department of Justice, responsible for investigating the breaking of Federal laws.

gravitational lens an object that has a strong gravitational pull

gravity the force of attraction between any two objects that have mass

Institute for Advanced Study research institute in Princeton, New Jersey, USA, founded in 1930

laser device for converting light of mixed frequencies into light waves of identical wavelength. A laser beam does not spread out like ordinary light waves and is therefore stronger.

mass the amount of matter in an object

matter anything that occupies space and has mass

molecule the smallest particle of an element or compound that normally exists on its own and still keeps its properties. Molecules usually consist of two or more atoms bound together.

Nazi member of the fascist National Socialist German Workers Party, which seized control in Germany in 1933

Nazism political creed followed by Nazis

Nobel Prize prize for outstanding contributions to chemistry, physics, physiology or medicine, literature, economics, and peace. It is awarded annually and was established in 1901 by Alfred Nobel.

nuclear energy energy released during a nuclear reaction

nucleus the central core of an atom, consisting of closely packed protons and neutrons

pacifist someone who believes that violence of any kind is unjustifiable, and that people should not take part in wars

particle minute amount of matter

particle accelerator machine for accelerating charged particles (protons and neutrons) to very high energies, used in nuclear physics to shatter atomic particles and provide information on their structure

patent grant to an inventor giving him or her the sole right to make, use and sell the invention for a fixed period of time

physiology the branch of science dealing with the way living things, or organisms, function

pulsar very small star which rotates fast, emitting pulses of radiation

quantum mechanics set of laws describing how atomic particles behave

quasar type of star that emits powerful radio waves and other forms of energy

radiation energy waves

species the specific group a plant or animal belongs to, within the larger genus or family group. It is the basic unit in the scientific classification system.

Weimar Republic the government that was founded in Germany in 1919 following the abdication of the Emperor

Zionism the movement that supported the claims of Jews who felt that a Jewish homeland should be established in the Middle East

Index